THE WAY WE WERE
NEW YORK

THE WAY WE WERE

NEW YORK

Nostalgic Images of the Empire State

M. J. Howard & Greg Dinkins

Guilford, Connecticut

gpp®

Design: Compendium Design/Angela and Dave Ball
Project manager: Martin Howard
Editor: Joshua Rosenberg
Contributing editor: Marcia Reiss
Photo credits: All photographs, unless specified below, are from the Library of Congress Prints & Photographs Division.
Corbis: 9 (Lake County Museum), 12 (Minnesota Historical Society), 16 (K.J. Historical), 10B (Lake County Museum), 21 (Lake County Museum), 28, 38L (Lucien Aigner), 38R (Hulton-Deutsch Collection), 40, 43 (Photo Collection Alexander Alland, Sr.), 44 (E.O. Hoppé), 45 (The Mariners' Museum), 50L, 58 (PoodlesRock), 59 (Photo Collection Alexander Alland, Sr.), 60 (Karen Tweedy-Holmes), 64 (Lucien Aigner), 65 (Lucien Aigner), 70 (Genevieve Naylor), 74 (Genevieve Naylor), 75 (Adrian Wilson/Beateworks), 76 (Genevieve Naylor), 79 (Bob Adelman), 86 (Aladdin Color, Inc.), 87 (Aladdin Color, Inc.), 89T (Michael Ochs Archives), 92R (Henry Diltz), 101T (Lake County Museum), 119T (Lake County Museum), 119B (Lake County Museum), 120TR (Jerry Cooke), 122–123 (Roger Wood), 124–125 (Cat's Collection), Corbis/Bettmann: 1, 2–3, 7, 13T, 15, 19, 30, 32, 33, 34–35, 36A, 37B, 46, 49, 53, 54L, 54, 66, 68, 69T, 69B, 71, 77, 78L, 83T, 83B, 84, 85, 88, 89B, 90L, 90R, 91T, 91B, 92L, 93, 94, 94–95, 95, 96TL, 96TR, 96B, 97, 99T, 99B, 100, 100B, 102, 104, 105T, 106, 107, 108T, 108B, 109, 110, 111T, 111B, 112T, 112B, 113, 114, 115B, 116, 117T, 120, 120TL, 120B, 121T, 121B, 122T, 122B, 123R, 124L, 125T, 125B, 126–127 Corbis/Schenectady Museum; Hall of Electrical History Foundation: 47, 48B, 52B, 56, 57, 72, 73, 103 Corbis/Underwood & Underwood: 39, 48T 50R, 51, 55, 105B, 118

Library of Congress Cataloging-in-Publication Data

Howard, M. J. (Martin J.)
  The way we were New York : nostalgic images of the Empire State / M.J. Howard & Greg Dinkins.
    p. cm.
  Includes index.
  ISBN 978-0-7627-5454-0
  1. New York (State)--History--20th century--Pictorial works. 2. New York (State)--Social life and customs--20th century--Pictorial works. I. Dinkins, Greg. II. Title.
  F120.R45 2009
  974.7'043--dc22

                                2009025343

Printed in China

10 9 8 7 6 5 4 3 2 1

CONTENTS

Introduction   6

1 New York Attractions   16

2 Making a State   40

3 New York at Home   60

4 New York at Play   80

5 New York Sport   98

6 A Special Place   116

Index   128

INTRODUCTION

The rich tapestry that is today's New York State owes everything to the people who have woven it over the years, from Native Americans to the often-forgotten everyday folk who have made their lives here, from frontiersmen, farmers, and cab drivers to merchant kings, celebrities, and philanthropists. For thousands of years the region belonged to native tribes. Archaeologists have identified signs of a sophisticated culture of self-sufficient people who made tools, hunted, fished, planted crops, traded among themselves, and developed complex spiritual beliefs. But their way of life changed forever in 1614 when the first Europeans settled here. No one could have imagined then how the landscape would be transformed by continuing waves of new arrivals. Over the centuries, generations of New Yorkers—descendants of people from every part of the world—have built an amazingly diverse state, a place of picturesque towns and villages as well as bustling

"If there were a god of New York, it would be the Greek's Hermes, the Roman's Mercury. He embodies New York qualities: the quick exchange, the fastness of language and style, craftiness, the mixing of people and crossing of borders, imagination."

Dr. James Hillman

cities, of farmland, industry, commerce, and astounding engineering achievements. We New Yorkers have been spoiled for things to do and see, with the big city for shows and shopping, history all around us at some of the earliest European settlements in the United States, and mountain resorts where we could get away from it all in summer or get our thrills on the winter slopes.

Looking around the state now it's almost impossible to imagine that all these things haven't always been here, but New York's evolution from wilderness to powerhouse has taken place over a relatively short space of time. It's been quite a journey for a state that only saw its

OPPOSITE: An immigrant family on the dock at Ellis Island, New York City, having passed the rigid examination for entry into the "land of promise," looks hopefully at the 1925 skyline while awaiting the government ferry to carry them to their new life.

LEFT AND BELOW: Outside of New York's larger cities are hundreds of smaller towns and villages such as Chatham, in Columbia County, depicted in this panorama (below) in 1886. In places like these life was much quieter. Most houses—like the Old Parsonage, seen at left—were made of distinctive clapboard. Like many other towns across the state, Chatham's original settlers were Dutch. But they were joined later by successive waves of new arrivals, first Quakers, then other nationalities as immigration swelled the state's population.

CHATHAM, N. Y.
1886.

BELOW: Buffalo around the time of the city's centenary and the 1901 Pan-American Exposition. By the time this scene was captured, the city was a hub of industry, an important center on the Erie Canal, and the eighth biggest city in the United States.

first European settlers turn up in the seventeenth century. To appreciate New York as it is today, it's worth glancing back at what has passed.

The first Dutch trading post was Fort Nassau (founded 1614), just outside where the state capital of Albany now stands, while Fort Amsterdam on Manhattan Island was founded in 1625.

The ease with which fur trappers could access the interior along the Hudson and Mohawk Rivers ensured that the settlements attracted early colonists, and Fort Amsterdam in particular soon grew into a somewhat wild place of woodsmen and seafarers with a full complement of merchants, smugglers, pirates, and rowdy taverns. Even in the earliest colonial days

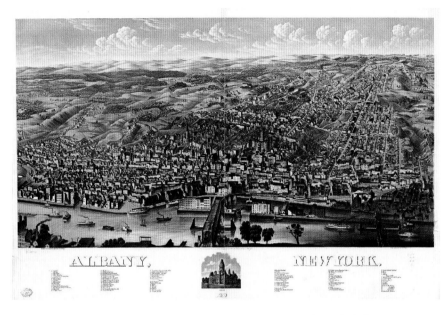

LEFT: This panoramic view of Albany dates to 1879. It's possible to see the large Capitol Building at the center of the thriving town, though the artist appears to have taken some license. The building was started in 1867, but not actually completed until twenty years after this panorama was drawn. It is interesting to note the size of the city harbor and the number of vessels on the river, a good indication of the volume of traffic plying the Hudson.

RIGHT: Albany became the permanent state capital in 1797 (before then the legislature shifted between Albany, Kingston, Poughkeepsie, and New York City). The current State Capitol—a distinctive mélange of the Renaissance and Romanesque styles—was declared open by Governor Theodore Roosevelt just over a century later.

OPPOSITE: Site of the first settlement in the original thirteen colonies, Albany can date its history back to the mid-sixteenth century. The original traders chose the site of their small fort wisely, and over the centuries the city slowly developed into an important transportation hub. By the mid-nineteenth century it was the United States' tenth most populous city.

the state was something of a melting pot. Although hostilities between colonials and Native Americans would spill over into King Philip's War in 1675 (so-called for Metacomet of the Wampanoag tribe, who was known as "Philip" by the English), there was a strong Native American presence across the region. Today something of the first inhabitants' heritage remains. There are seven federally recognized tribes in New York and nine reservations.

The Dutch may have been the first European settlers to arrive, but they weren't the last. The English were making incursions well before Britain seized New Amsterdam in 1664, renaming it New York in honor of the Duke of York. The fledgling city's first Jewish citizens arrived in 1654 and instantly took to the place. New York

City soon had the largest Jewish population in the colonies and many Jews served in the Continental Army during the American Revolution. During colonial times, a few free blacks managed to become landowners—one in Brooklyn as early as 1680—but they were the exception. Until slavery was abolished in New York State in 1827, enslaved Africans made up a substantial percentage of the population—nearly a third in the largely agricultural outreaches of Brooklyn. The large African-American community would later play an important role in the creation of the Underground Railroad, bringing escaped slaves to the Canadian border and freedom.

Early development was focused on Manhattan. The settlement's natural harbor and river links to the interior fed its growth into an important port and eventually the United States' first capital in 1788. As the city crept up Manhattan Island and spilled over into the boroughs, more and more people came: from Italy, Ireland, Germany, China, and everywhere else. From every corner of the globe they arrived—escaping oppression, fleeing famine, or just looking for a better life—flooding into the blossoming city and out across the state, swelling the population

ABOVE: Customers and butchers at the Albany Meat Market in the early twentieth century. The city started out as the region's first trading post, and its location on the Hudson River guaranteed that it remained an important market town as the state developed.

and adding their own distinctive cultures to the mix.

The diaspora from New York City to the rest of the state quickened when work on the Erie Canal began in the early nineteenth century. Irish immigrants, known as "bogtrotters," dug most of the canal, toiling in waist-deep muck and water, and many stayed after the canal opened up the West to profitable trade. Completed in 1825, the canal stretched across the state from Albany to Buffalo and turned all the villages along the way into cities: Troy, Schenectady, Amsterdam, Utica, Rome, Oneida, Syracuse, Rochester, and many

LEFT: As the state capital Albany has seen its share of political protest. In 1948 this band of demonstrators (including members of the Communist Party) marched from Albany's Union Station to the State Capitol on "Equal Rights Day" to press for anti-discrimination legislation, retention of the 5-cent New York subway fare, and—perhaps most important—a return of the nickel beer.

LEFT: Cornell University in Ithaca was founded in 1865 and has consistently upheld New York's intellectual reputation since. One of the world's top universities, it is a member of the illustrious Ivy League.

LEFT: At the time it was completed in 1902, the Flatiron Building at 23rd Street, Fifth Avenue, and Broadway was the tallest building in the world and an architectural wonder. Designed by Chicago's famous innovator Daniel Burnham, the triangular tower had the unsuspected effect of creating unusual wind currents that would frequently blow women's skirts up. This became such a well-known attraction that a policeman was placed outside permanently to move gawkers on, giving rise to the phrase "twenty-three skidoo."

barns and sightseers' delights, and eventually to a run of booming cities across the map.

By now the state had fully hit its pace. People continued to arrive at the immigration center on Ellis Island in the hundreds of thousands. They may have been drawn by Liberty's flame and the mythic status of the city, but beyond the skyscrapers were an abundance of prospects and possibilities. With its new highways, extensive rail network, humming electricity-generating stations, and booming factories, New York led the way into the future.

This book is a look back at some of the moments in New York's past that have been captured on canvas and film. Some of the scenes will be instantly familiar, while others show a more intimate side to the state. Yes, New York City looms large in the state's history and flavor, but there are other images here that take us beyond the skyscrapers and honking yellow cabs and into parts of New York less recognizable than the iconic city. While the images shown within these pages reflect long-ago events and places, they also embody what remains—the character and individuality of today's Empire State. This book shows the way we were in New York.

isolated settlements that didn't even have a stage line. Even Buffalo, located on Lake Erie, was in its infancy before the canal arrived and only afterward became a great port. Once the railroad connected more farms, towns, and villages, increasing trade and jobs, even more people spread across the state. This was the New York of *The Great Gatsby*, where trains and the subway could whip you from the heart of the Big Apple to sleek suburbia and roaring industry, beyond to farmland dotted with Dutch

ABOVE: Little Italy in the 1950s, a century after the first Italian immigrants settled in a triangle of Lower Manhattan wedged between Broadway and Houston, Canal, and Mulberry Streets. Today, Mulberry Street retains its Italian flavor in several legendary restaurants and bakeries.

NEW YORK ATTRACTIONS

"New York State: the state that has everything." It's as true now as it was in the 1920s when the poster to the right was printed. Back then, as today, when people thought of New York they thought of New York City. They needed reminding, perhaps, that New York doesn't end at the city limits of the Big Apple. Beyond the famous glass and concrete canyons lie more than 47,000 square miles. The state has 70,000 miles of rivers and streams; it borders two of the great lakes; it holds Atlantic beaches, historic towns and cities; and it has fairgrounds, caves, battle sites, museums, festivals, forests, and mountains. It has a history stretching back to the days of trappers and pirates, the iconic Statue of Liberty in New York Harbor, and the World's Tallest Uncle Sam at Lake George. New York State is awe-inspiring and absurd, modern and historic, dramatic and quaint. It's impossible to easily sum up this amazing place, but New York has a personality unlike anywhere else.

"New York had all the iridescence of the beginning of the world."

F. Scott Fitzgerald

LEFT: By the 1920s, when this poster was produced, visitors to New York had started turning their backs on the state's natural wonders and were drawn instead to the pleasures of the big city. They had to be reminded that New York also had many rural splendors to offer.

ABOVE: A view of tourists in the Catskill Mountains in the late 1800s. At that time New York's attractions were the serene landscapes of meadows, lakes, and waterfalls. Even then the tourist industry was large enough to support the two rural hotels shown here, and visitors could enjoy the views while promenading by the lake, hire a boat, or just take their ease at the elegant gazebo.

The tourist industry in New York has been in full swing since the mid-nineteenth century. In fact, the word "tourist" first appeared in American dictionaries as early as 1800, when it was used specifically to describe people flocking to New York to see its natural wonders. These days, the state welcomes roughly fifty million visitors a year and many of the attractions it has to offer now are the same that have lured visitors here since the nineteenth century. Back then, Niagara Falls often topped the list. Old photos of past visitors riding the *Maid of the Mist* beneath Horseshoe Falls convey a sense that very little has changed over the years.

New York City has striking examples of great architecture, to be sure, but so do many other cities throughout the state. While the Chrysler Building and the Empire State have proclaimed the city's architectural prominence since the 1930s, Buffalo residents more than a century ago could point with pride to major works by Frank Lloyd Wright, Louis Sullivan, Henry Hobson Richardson, and Daniel Burnham—and they still do. Once the railroads brought growth and prosperity throughout the state, small-town residents took just as much pride in their

handsome town halls, ornate music halls, and picturesque Victorian homes, many of which are preserved in National Historic Districts today. The nationally known landscape architects, Frederick Law Olmsted and Calvert Vaux, didn't confine their work to New York City's Central Park. Among their many achievements, one of the most innovative was Buffalo's park system, the nation's first interconnected network of parks and tree-lined parkways.

Opera, or something like it, was also enjoyed in both the big city and small towns throughout the state. In 1850, soprano Jenny Lind, the "Swedish Nightingale," drew thousands to her performances at Castle Garden, originally built in 1812 as a fort in Lower Manhattan. Promoted by impresario P. T. Barnum, she became a national sensation long before New York City built its first Metropolitan Opera House in 1883. Small towns throughout New York were already building their own "opera houses," more like music halls that hosted traveling performers, along with dress balls, church benefits, and high school graduations. The tiny village of Cambridge in northeastern New York

OPPOSITE: By the 1950s, Niagara had long been one of New York's most popular tourist attractions. Napoleon Bonaparte's brother visited in the early 1800s, acrobats including the famous Charles Blondin crossed it on a tightrope, daredevils launched themselves over the top in barrels, and in the nineteenth century it had already become a popular spot of choice for weddings and honeymoons.

LEFT: The Finger Lakes region of Central New York is one of America's great vacation spots. In this old postcard each letter shows a different local scene: F is Historical Canandaigua Court House; the I, General John Sullivan's Monument, near Waverly; N is Taughannock Falls, near Ithaca; G, Skaneateles Lake; E, the Historical Scythe Tree; R, Geneva Harbor on Seneca Lake; L, Famous Catharine Creek Trout Stream; A, Lucifer Falls in Robert Treman State Park, near Ithaca; K, the trail in Watkins Glen State Park; E, Sailboating on Keuka Lake; S, Harris Hill, Glider Capitol in Elmira.

ABOVE: In the early twentieth century Buffalo was a bustling city with some fine architecture. The Guaranty Building (now known as the Prudential Building) to the rear of St. Paul's Cathedral was the last building that Louis Sullivan and Dankmar Adler collaborated on. Across the street from the cathedral is the glorious Richardson Romanesque Erie County Bank Building, which was demolished in 1968.

ABOVE: The *Maid of the Mist* carrying 1940s sightseers beneath the roaring torrent of Horseshoe Falls, Niagara. Voyagers were swathed in oilskins as a defense against the saturating spray as they watched the spectacle of the mighty volume of water passing over the precipice 160 feet above. Visitors today enjoy the same thrilling ride.

still operates its own opera house, Hubbard Hall, built in 1878. A contemporary theater company now performs there, on the same stage where the writer and humorist Mark Twain, at one time an editor at the *Buffalo Express*, spoke on a statewide lecture tour.

Outdoor enthusiasts have been scaling mountain peaks in the Catskills and the Adirondacks since the mid-nineteenth century and hiking through thick forest along the Appalachian Trail since it was completed in 1937. As industrialization spread throughout the countryside after the Civil War, New York's unspoiled wilderness areas drew tourists in search of natural beauty and a healthier environment. Artists, particularly those of the Hudson River school, had discovered many of these areas and popularized them through their romantic landscape paintings.

To reach scenic, yet remote resorts like the Catskill Mountain House, built in 1823, tourists had to take a five-hour stagecoach ride up a 1,600-foot climb. The resort later built a cable-operated railway and the guests, including New York native President Theodore Roosevelt, kept coming until the late nineteenth century when the Catskills were eclipsed by the

ABOVE: New York has a host of architectural delights including the Fire Island Light, which once stood on the western edge of Fire Island in the days before accumulating sand made the island 6 miles longer. For many visitors crossing the Atlantic, the distinctive striped lighthouse would have been the first glimpse of America. It is now on the National Register of Historic Places.

Adirondacks as the fashionable playground of the wealthy. The Vanderbilts, Morgans, and other tycoons of the Gilded Age built Adirondack "Great Camps," rustic-styled estates with luxurious comforts. The wealthy and the rising middle class "took the waters" at several spas built around natural mineral springs in the state. The most famous was at Saratoga Springs, which also offered a casino and a racetrack, notably frequented by the most famous big spender of the Gilded Age, Diamond Jim Brady.

Once the automobile was on the roads, ordinary folks could venture to Central and Western New York State, touring the vineyards of the Finger Lakes region and the "Grand Canyon of the East" at Letchworth State Park. Some enjoyed visiting lighthouses, like the one in Buffalo, the oldest lighthouse on the Great Lakes, or exploring museums that ranged from the National Baseball Hall of Fame in Cooperstown to the Aquarium at Niagara. Many, no doubt, spent days antiquing and simply soaking up the atmosphere in New York's beautiful old towns and villages.

New York has always known how to entertain, too, in its amazing festivals, exhibitions, and events. Most famous was the Woodstock festival of 1969, which took place on Max Yasgur's Farm just outside Bethel, but the state has a rich tradition of special events. The Pan-American Exposition of 1901 was held in Buffalo, then known as the City of Light because the fair buildings were outlined in light bulbs electrified by energy generated by the nearby Niagara Falls. Unfortunately, the event is remembered as the place where President William McKinley was assassinated. The news reached his successor, Theodore Roosevelt, while he was vacationing at his family cabin on Mount Marcy, the tallest peak in the Adirondacks. He rode down the steep mountain trail by horse-drawn carriage in the dark, traveling all night to catch a train back to Washington. Today's New Yorkers have happier memories of the World's Fairs of 1939 and 1964 in Queens. And speaking of something for everyone, New York even has a history of rodeos, popular for years in many towns, perhaps most appropriately in Wyoming County. Yes, New York does have a Wyoming County, not surprisingly, in the western part of the state.

LEFT AND BELOW LEFT: Buffalo won the honor of hosting the 1901 Pan-American Exposition partly due to its prominence as a blossoming city with a population of over 350,000 people and partly due to its excellent rail links, which allowed millions to visit. The centerpiece of the fair, which lasted from May to November, 1901, was the magnificent Electric Tower that blazed with light at night. Other attractions of the fair included the Cardiff Giant display, American Inn, Lubin's Cineography, and streets of Cairo.

RIGHT: One of the best-known of New York's skyscrapers, the Woolworth Building was the world's tallest building when it opened on April 24, 1913. Sold to the Witkoff Group in 1998, it was designed by architect Gilbert Cass and built at a cost of $13,500,000.

ABOVE: The most beautiful building in the world? The Chrysler Building's Art Deco spire and its fine proportions certainly make it memorable. It is seen from the top of the Empire State Building in 1932. In the background is the Queensboro Bridge; completed in 1909, it connects Manhattan and Queens.

RIGHT: A much-changed skyline—Midtown New York looks relatively uncluttered in 1931. The recently completed Empire State Building—lacking its top mast—is at left; the Chrysler Building at right.

BELOW RIGHT: New York skyscrapers in 1916. In the foreground stands the Singer Building. Completed in 1908, it was demolished in 1968 in an act of cultural vandalism surpassed only by the earlier destruction of Penn Station in 1963.

OPPOSITE: Madison Square panorama in 1910—eight years after the Flatiron Building (at right) was completed. In the center, dominating the park, is the Met Life Tower, the tallest building in the world until the completion of the Woolworth Tower.

SARATOGA SPRINGS

Along with Niagara Falls, one of New York's earliest and biggest attractions was the town of Saratoga Springs. The town was first permanently settled in 1776, and floods of tourists began arriving soon after. The area has bounteous natural mineral springs, which were thought to have medicinal properties, and thousands flocked to benefit from the waters. Hotels, theaters, gardens, casinos, and parks soon sprang up, making Saratoga Springs one of the nation's first resort towns.

LEFT: Natural springs can be found all over Saratoga, and many have their own distinctive taste. While some were covered by simple pavilions, others grew into large spa hotels. You could even drink the waters at the station: as pictured, a boy serves stagecoach passengers.

LEFT: Saratoga Springs in the late eighteenth century, by which time the Grand Union Hotel on Broadway was the largest hotel anywhere in the world.

LEFT: Stagecoaches full of visitors arrive at one of Saratoga Springs' new hotels, circa 1889.

A National Historic Landmark since 1963, Central Park is one of New York City's great treasures. Although at points of its history the park has been neglected and badly maintained, since the 1980s it has been restored by a public-private partnership. Through good times and bad, it has always served its main mission—to provide New Yorkers a place to get away from the bustle of the streets and relax in a beautiful, carefully landscaped environment. On February 16, 1959, blizzards left Central Park under 10 inches of snow, providing perfect conditions for winter fun for the city's youngsters.

LEFT: A 1917 view of Lower East Side from Manhattan Bridge. In the background rises the Manhattan Municipal Building designed by McKim, Mead, and White and finished in 1915.

BELOW LEFT: A 1918 view of the Washington Square Arch. Originally a plaster and wood arch erected to mark the centennial of Washington's inauguration, the permanent structure was designed by Stanford White and completed in 1892. The statues of Washington were later (1918) additions. The photograph shows the funeral procession for John Purroy Mitchel—the youngest mayor of New York ever. His death owed more to farce than tragedy: he joined the U.S. Air Service after failing to be reelected and died after falling from his aircraft. He had forgotten to fasten his seatbelt.

OPPOSITE: With the Sherry-Netherland, Savoy Plaza, and Plaza Hotels as a backdrop, families kept cool in the hot summer of 1933 by boating on the Central Park pond, one of seven bodies of water in the park. The nineteenth century park designers created them all by draining and reshaping swamps.

RIGHT: No trip to New York would be complete without a trip to see "Lady Liberty" on Liberty Island in New York Harbor. A gift from the French people in 1886, the statue stands close to Ellis Island, the United States' center of immigration until 1954. She is particularly beloved by all those who saw her as the first glimpse of their new life in America. On this day in 1956 she was visited by a party from Brazil.

One of New York's many claims to fame, the Brooklyn Bridge was the longest in the world when completed in 1883. With its distinctive Gothic arches it is, like the Empire State Building, one of the most iconic and best loved parts of the skyline and has long been a favorite with visitors eager to cross its pedestrian walkway.

CONEY ISLAND

LEFT: Girl Scouts scream aboard one of Coney Island's famous roller coasters in 1949. The resort's amusement parks pioneered roller coasters. The first full-circuit coaster and the first lift-hill were both to be found here.

In the 1860s the Coney Island & Brooklyn Railroad streetcar line was completed and suddenly the beach was an affordable trip away, the perfect antidote to stifling summer days in the city. New Yorkers flocked to visit and businesses flocked to make a buck by providing them with entertainment. Over the following decades Coney Island became a vibrant resort, the perfect place for a date, and—with the opening of Nathan's in 1916—the birthplace of the hot dog.

BELOW: By the end of the nineteenth century Coney Island was a notorious den of vice, but with commercial success the resort gradually changed its reputation and by 1902 was a popular family destination.

ABOVE: In operation between 1904 and 1911, Dreamland was only one of Coney Island's amusement parks, the others including Steeplechase and Luna. The man behind Dreamland was the well-known (and crooked) New York businessman William H. Reynolds, who built a wonderland that included rides that were intended to impart Bible tales.

RIGHT: Many couples will remember nights spent courting on the beach at Coney Island, the perfect place for a date to remember.

THE EMPIRE STATE BUILDING

The centerpiece of New York's skyline since its completion in 1931, the Empire State Building is one of the world's most recognizable landmarks, the pride of the city, and was the tallest building in the world for forty years until the North Tower of the World Trade Center was completed in 1972. Since opening, well over 100 million people have ascended the building's high speed elevators to marvel at the view from the observation decks on the 86th and 102nd floors.

OPPOSITE, BOTTOM LEFT: New York City visitors take in the view from the Empire State Building's 86th-floor observation deck in 1941.

OPPOSITE, RIGHT: Enjoying the view from the Empire State Building in 1930. Left of the death-defying construction worker is the recently completed art deco Chrysler Building, another of New York City's iconic buildings.

RIGHT: The newly finished Empire State Building dwarfs its neighbors and dominates the Manhattan skyline. Completed just as the Great Depression started, finding occupants for its high-priced offices proved so difficult that for its early years New Yorkers nicknamed it the "Empty State Building."

MAKING A STATE

When visitors walk through New York's sleepy upstate villages, it's hard for them to imagine that the state has always been at the cutting edge of new development. Whenever revolutions—transportation, agricultural, urban, technological—have swept the world, the Empire State was among the first to adopt and innovate, not just in New York City, but across the state. As New Yorkers have known since the first trappers and traders founded a trading post on the Hudson River, the secret to success is infrastructure. They were lucky enough to have an easy-to-navigate conduit from the abundant hunting grounds of the interior to the coast, and—at Fort Amsterdam on the tip of Manhattan Island—a natural harbor where ships awaited to transport their wares to Europe and its insatiable market for fur, particularly beaver pelt. It was an obvious port of call for cross-Atlantic traffic as well as for ships plying the Eastern Seaboard, allowing New Amsterdam to zoom from a tiny settlement to a bustling

"Ideas matter in New York. I am certain that more conversations in New York are about ideas than anywhere else. Not just vague theories, but ideas that New Yorkers have the will, and the clout, to do something about."

David Frost

ABOVE: Construction of the massive Catskill Aqueduct began in 1907 and lasted until 1924. The aqueduct transports water from the Catskill Mountains to Yonkers where it is piped to individual towns and cities. These workers had just begun blasting the rocky base of the Hudson River in 1912. The 163-mile system would eventually include three dams and sixty-seven shafts.

village and then a major town. Since then the state has gone from strength to strength, providing its citizens with great schools, universities, and hospitals as well as planes, trains, automobiles, roads, bridges, and tunnels that help whip people and goods to where they need to be at a speed those first settlers could never have imagined.

The lessons of the first colonists weren't lost on their descendants or new arrivals to the state. Although the first century and a half of New York's existence saw its population rise from a handful of Europeans to tens of thousands of people, there was still fierce competition from ports such as Boston and Philadelphia farther up the coast. New Yorkers knew that they had to develop their transportation and communication network to keep ahead of the game.

Their typically ambitious response was the Erie Canal, which was completed in 1825 and linked the Hudson to Lake Ontario, connecting New York to the farmlands of the West. The canal ran 365 miles from Albany to Buffalo and opened up vast new areas of the interior. Now, there was a much quicker, cheaper way of transporting goods across the great

RIGHT AND BELOW: From the earliest days New York was a busy agricultural state. When the Erie Canal and, later, the railways opened up new markets to the east, companies like Jerome B. Rice & Co. made a profit from selling seeds to a new generation of pioneering farmers.

RIGHT: Situated in Oneida County, stemming the flow of the Mohawk River, is the Delta Lake Dam. Construction of the dam began in 1908 and its completion heralded the end for the small town of Delta, which once lay on the west bank of the Mohawk and was drowned by the 20.6 billion gallons of water that the new dam collected.

ABOVE LEFT: Situated on the eastern shore of Lake Erie, Buffalo began life as a small trading community. By 1900, thanks to the Erie Canal, it had blossomed into America's eighth largest city and a major manufacturing and shipping center.

LEFT: Albany was ideally situated to become a major hub of transportation even before the arrival of the Erie Canal, but like Buffalo it enjoyed greatly increased prosperity after the new waterway was completed.

distances of continental North America than the horse and cart. As the great port at the end of the line, New York City reaped most of the benefits, though the canal also spurred migration from the city to the western part of the state, leading to a huge increase in Buffalo's population and catalyzing economic growth in towns all along the route. For early nineteenth century New York, it was a massive undertaking and, rightly, known as the "Eighth Wonder of the World." New Yorkers have had a great affection for the canal ever since and have even celebrated it in song and literature. These days it is no longer a major transportation artery, but many sections have been designated National Historic Landmarks and attract large numbers of tourists.

In 1831, just a few years after the Erie

Canal was completed, New York witnessed a technological marvel when one of the first steam engines in America puffed along the rails of the Mohawk & Hudson line, where only draft animals had pulled trolleys in the past. The *DeWitt Clinton* locomotive, ironically named for the New York governor who was the "Father of the Erie Canal," led a transportation revolution that eventually made the canal obsolete. Playing to a packed crowd along the length of the 17-mile run from Albany to Schenectady, the engine pulled three passenger coaches filled with people who were bounced and

FAR LEFT: A boat passes below the massive grain elevators bordering the Erie Canal at Buffalo in 1926. This one image encapsulates the keys to New York's success: engineering know-how and a route to the vast resources of the continent.

LEFT: The southern tip of Manhattan in 1923. At the feet of the city's towers lay sources of New York's wealth: ferry terminals that brought tens of thousands to work in the city's financial and shipping center in Lower Manhattan, alongside huge docks that served merchant ships from around the globe.

OPPOSITE: New Yorkers have always found their own uses for the city's infrastructure. At 65th Street and the East River, young Manhattanites used the dock as a springboard into the river during the 1948 heat wave.

RIGHT: The forerunners of the elevated railway and subway were trolley buses, and a number of cities in New York adopted them as their first public transport systems. The first streetcar line (in the state and in the world) was the New York and Harlem Railroad's Fourth Avenue Line, which began service in 1832. Its success sparked the opening of many more lines that were popular for many decades until the new subway made them obsolete.

bumped in cars made from old horse carriages mounted on railroad trucks held together by chain. They emerged battered and bruised at the end of the line, but nevertheless it was a historic moment in New York's history and the people of the state began building tracks with gusto.

Within a few short years, railways such as the Utica & Schenectady and the Syracuse & Utica were proliferating, and a web of lines slowly spread across the state.

By 1853, they had come together as the New York Central Railroad. The railway had truly arrived, and with it the age of brakemen and hobos, of puffing high speed travel and massive new economic success, of new towns and great stations such as Pennsylvania and Grand Central.

New York City soon adopted rail travel to the outlying boroughs of the ever-expanding city, at first on elevated

rails, but eventually going beneath the ground. Following the example of the London Underground in England, Alfred Ely Beach opened his Beach Pneumatic Transit beneath Broadway in 1869. The city loved the idea, for by this time the streets of New York were becoming jammed with traffic, but the expense of building the subway system proved prohibitive. It wasn't until 1904 that the first part of the original subway opened, offering service between City Hall and the Bronx. Over the following decades the city overcame financial hurdles to construct one of the most extensive underground rail systems in the world.

And though city-dwelling New Yorkers—especially Manhattanites—have long preferred hailing a cab (the first taxi company was formed in 1907) or using the subway to buying a car of their own, the state has never lagged behind in building roads. In fact, New York began building highways early and, after the federal government offered construction grants in 1916, had its first modern highways as early as the Twenties.

Another of New York's many firsts is the adoption of electricity for domestic

ABOVE: "The new type" of streetcar by General Electric, which was foot controlled and allowed the driver to navigate in "ease and comfort." Streetcars were a common sight in the cities of Buffalo, Albany, Schenectady, Yonkers, and Rochester, and in all of them the lines served the public until after World War II.

BELOW: New York's preeminence as a state is largely due to its excellent transport links. Citizens such as the group in this late nineteenth century photo were eager to take advantage of new advances. Introduced in the mid-1880s, the *De Witt Clinton* train provided the first passenger rail service from Albany to Schenectady, and was only the third of these locomotives in the nation.

use. In 1882, Thomas Edison switched on the world's first electric power station at Pearl Street, New York City, and instantly provided his fifty-nine customers with electric light. Within a few years the whole city was ablaze, and soon after, the rest of the state, too. Electricity sizzled up and down Broadway, giving New York its first taste of glitter and helping to create that dazzling nighttime skyline.

Electricity isn't the only area in which New York has been forward-looking.

Thanks to the creativity and good sense of its citizens, the city has been providing its inhabitants with fresh water along the Old Croton Aqueduct since 1842. These days the state brings over a billion gallons of water into homes each day from the Catskills. Today New York City is one of only five cities in the United States that has pure drinking water of a standard that needs little filtration or purification. And in these environmentally conscious days when people are urged to "eat local," New York

ABOVE: New York City's Sixth Avenue circa 1940 with an elevated train above the crowded street. Elevated trains began running in the 1870s, quickly becoming a clattering part of New York City's background hum. Many lines survived the opening of the subway and are still part of the system today. The oldest length of track still in use dates to 1885.

RIGHT: Workers excavating the subway system in New York City wait at the Canal Street Shaft and Air Locks, South Tunnel. Some workers at this stretch of the tunnel labored in hour-and-a-half shifts in pressurized tubes beneath the East River, and—like divers—needed decompression before returning to the surface.

5476

also has a "local food shed" that encourages sustainable, responsible farming.

As you might expect for the state where the Wright brothers made the first flight around the Statue of Liberty (1909) and where aviation pioneer Glenn Curtiss was born, New York has also been at the forefront of air travel. Albany's airport was the first in the United States, Buffalo had its own by 1926, and by the 1950s every city from Binghamton to Utica was welcoming air traffic.

The list of New York achievements also includes public services (New York's firefighters and police departments are

ABOVE: Like the docks, the subway provided unforeseen opportunities for fun. This photograph shows youngsters fishing for money lost by pedestrians, which had rolled through the subway gratings. With the aid of a stick, a piece of twine, and some sticky pieces of gum, there was a fortune to be made!

justly famed around the globe), schools and universities, state parks, and libraries. In more ways than most people realize, New York has set the pace for the rest of the world and defined itself as a place that is always ahead of the times.

CITY OF NEW YORK
MUNICIPAL AIRPORTS
NO.1 FLOYD BENNETT FIELD · NO. 2 NORTH BEACH
EAST RIVER SEAPLANE BASES   WALL STREET — 31ˢᵗ STREET
F.H.LaGUARDIA   JOHN McKENZIE
MAYOR   COMMISSIONER OF DOCKS

LEFT: A poster in the art deco style dating from the Thirties advertises Floyd Bennett Field, New York City's first municipal airport, located in Brooklyn. It opened in 1930 and though it no longer serves as an airport, some of its buildings remain and are on the National Register of Historic Places. Facing the ocean-front, it attracts migrating birds and is also part of National Gateway Park.

OPPOSITE, BOTTOM: Although his achievements are less famous than those of the Wright brothers, New Yorker Glenn Curtiss was a pioneering engineer who set the pace for the state to become a world leader in aviation. Having become the "Fastest Man on Earth" in 1907 on a motorcycle of his own design, he turned his attention to aircraft and on May 29, 1910, flew from Albany to New York City along the Hudson River, winning a $10,000 prize. Along with his many other honors, Curtiss was the first person to be awarded a U.S. pilot's license (the Wrights followed with numbers four and five).

ABOVE: Since the first commercial flight landed there in 1948, John F. Kennedy Airport has welcomed millions of people from all over the world to the state, few more famous than these four young men, the Beatles, who arrived in 1964.

ABOVE: With many more cars on the roads of New York City in the early twentieth century, there was a pressing need to keep traffic moving. This task fell to a new breed of police officer: the traffic cop. Captured on camera in the early Thirties, this officer is directing cars with a whistle and hand signals at 135th Street and Lenox Avenue in Harlem.

ABOVE: Roads also meant motels and gas stations, both of which sprung up along the highways. Edith Crognale of Ossining ran the Garden Gas Station at Albany Post Road and Highland Avenue with her mother.

LEFT: Bumper to bumper traffic on 59th Street between Second and Third Avenues. From the days that cars were first seen on city streets, New York City has never been a place for drivers who like the freedom of the open road.

THE GENERAL ELECTRIC COMPANY

Schenectady, home to the headquarters of the General Electric Company from 1892 and to the American Locomotive Company from 1901, was known as "The City That Lights and Hauls the World." Started by Thomas Edison, G.E. expanded exponentially as New York switched on to the new form of power, creating a vast complex of generators and engineering and administration offices.

RIGHT: The General Electric Company provided the Schenectady area with many employment opportunities, including jobs for women working at the headquarter's telephone switchboard.

RIGHT: Schenectady was quick to adapt the new technologies being developed in its backyard to local public services. These lucky young students at the state-of-the-art Riverside School had a classroom equipped with automatic light control.

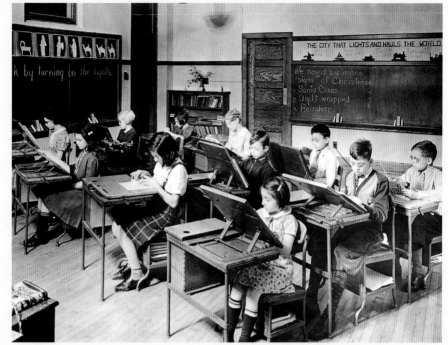

BELOW: The enormous General Electric Company buildings in the early twentieth century.

LEFT AND BELOW LEFT: Over the years New York has had numerous reasons to be proud of its fire department. In the early days of the twentieth century you could buy postcards of the firefighters showing off their new "Auto Hook and Ladder" equipment. Even during the 1936 ice storm (below), New York firefighters could be counted on to overcome a blaze.

OPPOSITE: The first fire hydrant was introduced in 1908, and since then cooling down in a hydrant's spray during the city's long, hot summers has become a tradition.

NEW YORK AT HOME

New York has come a long way since its early settlers constructed primitive wooden shacks to keep off the elements. Since then, its citizens have lived in homes of almost every conceivable fashion, from grand country estates and clapboard cottages to loft apartments and cramped tenements. Many of the state's houses are veritable architectural wonders and now appear on the National Register of Historic Places. The list is long and as varied as Frank Lloyd Wright's Darwin D. Martin House in Buffalo, a prime example of Wright's revolutionary Prairie House designs, and the unusual domed octagonal Armour-Stiner House in Irvington, Westchester County. From colonial styles through neoclassical, to suburban ranch-style houses or the sleek lines of the international style, New York's homes are as varied and full of character as the people who have lived in them over the years.

The early settlers brought with them the designs of their own countries,

"The exodus from New York City limits to the suburbs in the last two decades was nothing less than spectacular and probably represents one of the greatest unattended migrations in human history."

Dave Marash

ABOVE: Huguenot settlers fled religious persecution and discrimination in France and settled in New Paltz, New York, which remains one of the oldest communities in America. Distinctive stone houses such as this one were built in the eighteenth century.

marking the state with beautiful examples of early American architecture based on European precedents. Many parts of upstate New York offer a rich flavor of how America's ancestors lived in the early days of colonial settlement. The Pieter Bronck House (1663) still stands just south of Albany as the oldest extant building in upstate New York. The Huguenot Street Historic District in New Paltz includes a particularly fine example of Hudson Valley Dutch architecture in its eighteenth century Jean Hasbrouck House. And the Geneseo Historic District is a beautifully preserved collection of nineteenth century homes, churches, and libraries. But as the state became an industrial and mercantile powerhouse, the simple styles of the "old country" gave way to homes that reflected the growing nation and its increasingly diverse population. From palaces on Fifth Avenue to country mansions, brownstones, and apartment buildings, New York helped blaze the trail for a country meeting its own needs and finding its own

ABOVE: The oldest building in upstate New York, the Pieter Bronck House was built in 1663. It was here that the Coxsackie Declaration of Independence was signed in 1775.

LEFT: The city of Newburgh, Orange County, boasts many fine examples of nineteenth century architecture, especially along Montgomery, Grand (pictured), and Liberty Streets, which have now been incorporated in a protected historic district.

OPPOSITE, TOP: Long before the immigration center opened on Ellis Island, New York was welcoming people escaping from persecution in their native lands. This old Shaker house was in Mount Lebanon, Columbia County, the spiritual home of the Shaker community after they first arrived in New York City in 1776.

OPPOSITE, BOTTOM: Buffalo is the home of Frank Lloyd Wright's Darwin D. Martin House. One of the best examples of the great architect's "Prairie School" of design, which attempted to provide the United States with its own form of domestic architecture, it is held to be the pinnacle of Wright's early career.

architectural personality. Booming urban populations demanded homes that took full advantage of small building lots. One answer was closely packed row-houses, which proliferated in the cities from the beginning of the eighteenth century. Originally made from wood or brick, homes for the rising middle classes reflected their desire for more sophisticated materials. The city's builders responded by constructing rowhouses with sandstone found in nearby quarries.

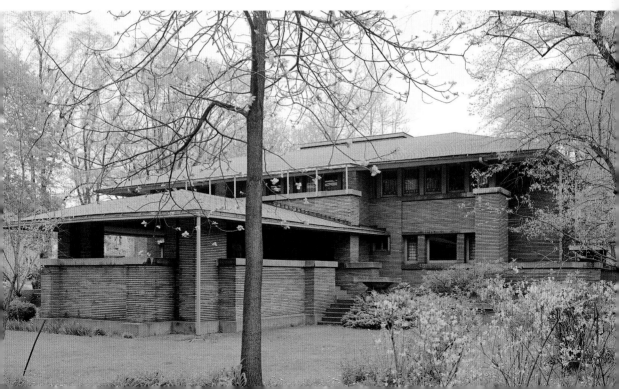

ABOVE: New York City's rowhouses were usually built with servants' quarters below and steps leading up to the main entrance. These provided an excellent place for locals to sit and watch the world go by.

OPPOSITE: A group of men and women cook together at a communal kitchen in Harlem during the Great Depression.

Dark brown in color, it gave the city its distinctive and much loved "brownstones." Another answer was to go upward. Tenement buildings with families crammed into tiny apartments over several floors had been a feature of New York City's architecture since 1839, when the first was built, but the famous Dakota Building, which opened in 1884, introduced Manhattan to the idea of luxury apartments. Other cities in the state were quick to follow suit. Buffalo, for example, still has some wonderful examples, such as the Colonial Apartments (1896) and the charming art deco Bennett Apartments dating to the Thirties.

New York City also led the way in housing for the poor. In 1934, in the midst of the Great Depression, Mayor Fiorello La Guardia established the first public housing authority in the country. Nearly eighty years later, hundreds of thousands of people in the five boroughs have a roof over their heads thanks to the New York City Housing Authority.

As the spread of the railways and roads offered a quick route into New York City from outlying areas, so the country's biggest commuter belt came into existence. The Tri-State Region

(which includes parts of New Jersey and Connecticut) is these days the biggest metropolitan region in the United States. About one in sixteen of all Americans live within commuting distance of the Big Apple. After World War II, thousands of GIs returning to New York looked beyond the city limits for homes for their growing families. They found what they were looking for in Levittown, Long Island, built in 1947 by the Levitt and Sons Company. It was the second planned suburban community in the country (the first was San Lorenzo Village in California) and instantly successful. By the following year, affordable, comfortable houses were going up at the rate of thirty a day. The idea was copied again and again, and Levittown is now considered such an important part of American history that the Smithsonian is acquiring a Levittown exhibit, including an entire house.

These modern homes were equipped with mass-produced furniture and all the latest gadgets. By now, only the most remote homes were without electricity. Vacuum cleaners, washing machines, and—later—dishwashers were revolutionary ways to lighten the load of

RIGHT: Even by 1947, many people outside the cities still lived a simpler existence in homes like this two-room wooden shack in Oniontown. According to the notes attached to the photograph, owner Richard Wilcox was more than happy not to have the intrusions and worries of a more modern life.

household chores and allowed families more leisure time to listen to the radio, watch their new televisions, or just play ball in the backyard.

Whether a downtown apartment or a historic country house, the homes of New York offer an interesting glimpse into the lives of its people and its history. In the places they have lived, it's possible to see the tenacity of early settlers, the opulence of the mighty tycoons, the ambitions of city dwellers, and the simple joy of family life common to all New Yorkers.

LEVITTOWN

Although it was preceded by a planned community in California, Levittown is often thought of as the first truly mass-produced suburb and was much copied around the state and the country. Where fields of potatoes had been tilled for a century, Levitt and Sons built modern, affordable homes at an incredible rate. They proved so popular that the 2,000 homes planned in 1947 increased to just under 17,500 by 1951. Alongside these were schools, shops, and everything else the families that flocked here could need.

RIGHT: An aerial view of Levittown in 1949. The thousands of houses all looking the same may not have been everyone's idea of a great place to live, but they were cheap, comfortable, and offered an easy commute into the city.

OPPOSITE, BOTTOM RIGHT: Some of Levittown's first residents take advantage of the shopping opportunities. The advertising literature for Levittown homes was at pains to point out the convenience, the plentiful parking spaces, and the beautiful wide, tree-lined streets.

LEFT: A typical Levittown street in 1954. Often criticized for its blandness, the town was well liked by most of those who made their homes here, and some notable names grew up on its streets, including singer Billy Joel.

LEFT: As many families moved away from the city and settled in the suburbs—in this case Long Island—they were introduced to the delights of having a yard of their own in which children could play. Shooting hoops was a popular pastime back then as it is today.

OPPOSITE: New York's television services (the first non-experimental transmissions in the country) started in 1928 with infrequent broadcasts from New York City and GE headquarters in Schenectady. Three years later the W2XAB station in the city began a regular seven-day-a-week service. By 1939 there were about 2,000 sets in the state and the number tripled over the following three years until World War II put an end to production for a while. Nevertheless, when hostilities ended, New Yorkers took to TV with even greater enthusiasm, and by the Fifties TV sets were a fixture of most New York homes.

OPPOSITE AND RIGHT: As well as producing electricity, the General Electric Company in Schenectady also manufactured new gadgets for the home that revolutionized the lives of New Yorkers far ahead of those in other parts of the country. The Schenectady Museum has a trove of photographs dating to the late 1930s, which show gadgets and gizmos that the company was pioneering. In these examples a mother makes lemonade for her daughter using an electric juicer (right) and a Schenectady housewife demonstrates a vacuum cleaner in the Home Electric show living room (opposite).

LEFT AND OPPOSITE: New York City apartments have been the epitome of chic living since the Dakota opened in 1884, though tastes changed from the austere elegance of the 1940s to the rather more flamboyant designs of the 1970s and later.

OPPOSITE: Although most New Yorkers were happy to embrace the future, some decided the old ways were best. Although she looks as though she would be at home in 1860, this lady lived on her old barge moored on the Hudson as recently as 1960.

ABOVE: Marine corporal Sidney Oehl surrounded by relatives in Brooklyn after serving in Korea. New York's homes have witnessed some momentous causes for celebration over the years, but there is none greater than welcoming a son safely home from war, especially in this case when he had been mistakenly reported as killed in action.

RIGHT: Those children whose backyards were the streets of New York City learned to improvise their play. The rungs of a fire escape ladder made a serviceable impromptu basketball hoop.

FAR RIGHT: By 1966, times were still tough for some families. This scene, of a large family living in a three-room apartment in Harlem, will be familiar to many who passed their childhood in the less affluent parts of the city.

NEW YORK AT PLAY

As people have been finding out for centuries, New York offers unlimited opportunities for fun. For those who prefer to spend their leisure time outdoors, snowy winters in upstate mountains are great for skiing and snowboarding, while warm summers bring boaters and anglers to the state's beautiful lakes and sunbathers to its beaches. The cities have countless restaurants, nightclubs, theaters, concert halls, museums, and diversions of every description, including some of the best shopping on the planet. You can take your pick of festivals and carnivals, or soak up the atmosphere of historic villages. In fact, if you can't have a good time in New York, then you probably can't have a good time anywhere.

Over the years inventive New Yorkers have found many ways to have a good time, but in the earliest days, most people were too busy trying to make a living in the New World to find time for recreation. Even children worked all day like

"Well, little old Noisyville-on-the-Subway is good enough for me."

O. Henry

RIGHT: Lyman Hakes Howe made a name for himself throughout New York State with his "High Class Moving Pictures," shown in small towns and church halls. But as the popularity of moving pictures grew, so did his venues. After starting as a small-time traveling showman, by 1903 he was the head of a successful tour company and had permanent bookings in theaters and opera houses.

adults. But as New York City grew more successful and new settlers began to appear, numerous taverns opened (about 150 by 1750), as well as the first coffee house—the King's Arms—which opened on Broadway in 1694. Drinking and simple games were for many the main source of entertainment throughout the area in

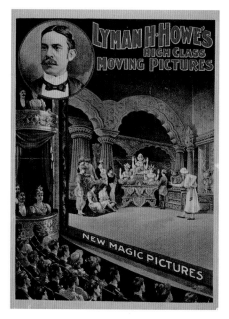

ABOVE: Unable to afford tickets for the movies,
Troy's youngsters peeked through the stage door,
setting a trend for kids of generations to come.

BELOW: The town of Huntington on the north coast of Long Island has long boasted a vibrant artistic scene. In 1917 the Rosemary Open-Air Theater hosted rehearsals for the annual National Red Cross Pageant.

the early years, but in Manhattan at least, there were soon more sophisticated pleasures to be had. Actors had probably been visiting New York as far back as the beginning of the 1700s, but the first proper theater was built in 1750. It is difficult to say with accuracy, but the Theatre on Nassau Street (close to Broadway in Lower Manhattan), as it was named, may have been the first in the country, and if not, it was one of the first. What is certain is that by this time the city had a population of around 10,000 and many now had money to spend and free time to enjoy themselves. And in New York the prevailing attitude was somewhat more laid back

04397

LEFT: The staff of Savage's Hotel and Casino in High Hill Beach pose for a group photograph. High Hill Beach was popular with tourists as it had a reputation for being very relaxed about Prohibition laws. The entire resort was torn down in 1939 and became Jones Beach State Park.

ABOVE: Competition judges Selig Rocheiser and Nils Grantlund take the measurements of Myra Stevens, runner-up in the "Modern Venus Contest 1937" at Steeplechase Park, Coney Island.

LEFT: A young family takes advantage of the mild summer in the mountains and the picture-perfect scenery of the Catskills to picnic at Lake Minnewaska in 1952.

ABOVE: In urban areas parks provided the best opportunity for play—and what better entertainment on a sunny day than the swings? Here, children in Hamilton Fish Park on the corner of Pitt and East Houston Street in Manhattan's Lower East Side.

ABOVE RIGHT: Camping has long been a favorite New York pastime. After a long week in the hustle and bustle of the cities, many people found that a weekend under canvas in the state's great outdoors was the perfect way to unwind. These two romantics are pictured at their camping ground overlooking Schroon Lake in the Adirondacks around 1950.

than elsewhere in the colonies, where Puritans still frowned on many of the popular entertainments of the day. When the English ousted the Dutch, they installed a succession of aristocratic governors who attempted to re-create the busy social lifestyle they had become used to at home. Among the *beau monde* of New York's major towns, and particularly New York City itself, the eighteenth century was a time of frivolity, costume balls, and concerts.

In the nineteenth century the opportunities for entertainment really blossomed. With economic success came an

LEFT: Many city-dwellers who wanted more conveniences than camping out offered could find them at the lakeside resorts around the state. At Capri Village on Lake George in the Sixties, holiday-makers could hire boats, rent a cabin, and just enjoy the sunshine.

ABOVE: The pleasures of New York aren't all about glitz and razzmatazz. As this group of young visitors to the Edgemere House Resort in Greene County found out, an evening hayride on an old-time ranch was just as much fun as anything the big city had to offer.

appetite for new diversions and across the state theaters, upscale hotels, and pleasure palaces were built. One of the most amazing spectacles was P. T. Barnum's entertainment complex in Lower Manhattan, which attracted thousands of visitors beginning in 1841. Here New Yorkers and tourists alike could stroll in rooftop gardens, take a ride in a hot air balloon, or be amazed by the exhibits and live performers. Booming Buffalo had its own theater district, which catered to both blue-collar workers and the city's tycoons, while even smaller towns boasted theaters or improvised with summer open-air amateur performances. Restaurants proliferated too. Delmonico's was one of the first in the country when it opened at 23 William Street, New York City, in 1827, and it was so successful that others soon sprung up. By 1859, the *New York Times* was running a restaurant review, and over the next few decades New Yorkers were spoiled for choice in restaurants of every kind across the state, including Jack's Oyster Bar in Albany from 1913 onward, and the first Chinese restaurants in the Big Apple's Chinatown, which opened around the same time.

In 1896, the first moving pictures to be seen in the United States were screened at Koster and Bial's Music Hall in New York City. New Yorkers took to the amazing new technology instantly. In the same year, the first theater in the world dedicated solely to showing movies opened in the basement of Buffalo's Ellicott Square Building.

Elsewhere in the state new entertainments were opening, notably Albany's New York State Museum, which opened its doors in 1836, the Buffalo and Erie County Botanical Gardens in 1868, and the Buffalo Zoo in 1875.

During the twentieth century, the leisure industry reached even greater heights. Notwithstanding Prohibition (which many New Yorkers ignored), the Great Depression, and two wars, the

ABOVE: The bright lights of Broadway have mesmerized visitors since the turn of the century. Some of the greatest stars have appeared on Broadway's stages over the years, including Judy Garland at Loew's State Theater in 1938.

ABOVE: The Cotton Club in Harlem was probably the most famous nightspot in New York City. Located in the heart of the African-American neighborhood and featuring some of the most talented black entertainers of the time on its bill—from Billie Holliday and Ella Fitzgerald to Count Basie and Cab Calloway—the club generally did not allow African-American patrons to enter, a reminder that for all its diversity New York still had a long way to go in treating all its citizens equally.

RIGHT: While audiences were listening to jazz and blues in Harlem, on Broadway they could find more extravagant entertainment. Probably the most famous show in town for over two decades—from 1907 until 1931, when the Great Depression forced it off stage—were the Ziegfeld Follies. These were flamboyant stage revues that featured provocatively (for the time) dressed dancers as well as some of the day's greatest entertainers.

state maintained its reputation as a place where a good time was guaranteed for all. A new wave of African-American migrants from the South brought jazz with them, beginning the age of big bands, nightclubs, and jitterbugging. With its famous Colored Musicians Club, Buffalo became a focus for some of the greatest African-American artists of the day. Meanwhile, audiences everywhere flocked to extravagant stage shows in theaters around the state.

A good time of a different kind could be found out in the countryside. The Appalachian Trail was slowly completed throughout the Thirties and Forties while ski resorts sprung up in the mountains. Even the weather couldn't stop the fun; in 1952 Grossinger's Resort in the Catskills became the first in the world to make artificial snow. A complete list of the events New York State now hosts each year would be far too long to include here, but it includes the Tulip Festival in Albany, jazz and arts festivals in most of the major

ABOVE LEFT: New Yorkers have always been able to have a good time wherever they find themselves, whether in a swanky casino or on a step in Brooklyn.

ABOVE: Central Park is a favorite for skaters winter or summer. These days you're most likely to see inline skaters sweeping along the paths, but back in the Seventies the craze was for roller skates.

ABOVE: Since the earliest days of the colonists, New Yorkers have enjoyed taking their ease at the local tavern. Even Prohibition made little impact, with the city boasting a multitude of speakeasies. These Harlem fight fans were caught on camera while celebrating after listening to the battle between Joe Louis and Germany's Max Schmeling on the wireless in 1938 (Louis won in the first round).

RIGHT: With so many different cultures mixing in New York, it was inevitable that the city would become a great place to eat out. From Japanese sushi to French *haute cuisine*, New York has boasted some of the best restaurants in the world since the first—Delmonico's—opened in 1827. Despite the great choice available, New Yorkers have always had a particularly soft spot for Italian, as these pedestrians on Broadway reveal in 1937.

ABOVE: New York City is famous, too, for its extravagant nightclubs, and no place was more exclusive than the Playboy Club, which opened in 1962. Those lucky enough to get in would be waited on by the famous Playboy bunnies who might have included Debbie Harry of rock band Blondie—a bunny from 1968 to 1973, Lauren Hutton (1963–64), and even the feminist writer Gloria Steinem (1963), who took the job as an undercover reporting assignment.

ABOVE: New York hosts many festivals each year, but undoubtedly the most famous was 1969's Woodstock. The musical jamboree took place just outside of Bethel in Sullivan County on Max Yasgur's dairy farm, which he rented to event organizers for $75,000. About 450,000 people attended the three-day concert, which turned into chaos due to the crowds, heavy rains, and traffic jams. Performing for the mud-soaked crowd were some of the greatest artists of the Flower Power generation, including the Grateful Dead; Crosby, Stills, Nash, and Young; Janis Joplin; and Jimi Hendrix. The festival is now remembered as the high point of the hippie age.

OPPOSITE: Another famous New York event is the annual Thanksgiving Day Parade, which was started in 1924 by Louis Bamberger's store in Newark, New Jersey, 1924, and quickly adopted for the city by Macy's department store. Since then it has become a time-honored part of the festive season, featuring Macy's employees dressed in costume, bands, animals, and huge balloons floating above. By the 1930s over a million people lined the streets annually to watch the parade pass by.

cities, and monthly art exhibits in Kingston, and the National Buffalo Wing Festival in—where else—Buffalo.

New York may have made its name in industry, transport, and business, but this is a state that knows how to enjoy itself.

SWINGING NEW YORK

Big swing bands were popular everywhere before and after World War II, but none of them swung like those in New York City. Developing from jazz in the Twenties and Thirties, it was the hot new music that pulled people onto the dance floor. Its fans developed new, energetic dances like the "Lindy Hop," the forerunner of jitterbugging and jiving, as the music swept the nation. As always, New York was at the epicenter. Although dance clubs and ballrooms could be found throughout the United States, probably the most famous of them all was the Savoy in Harlem.

RIGHT: Dressed in their best for an evening out in 1952, a Harlem crowd gathers for a photograph after dancing the night away to the sounds of trumpet player Erskine Hawkins and the Terry Gibbs Orchestra at the Savoy.

BELOW: Even smaller venues packed in customers eager to swing. This band played the Hickory House, a "swing salon" on 52nd Street.

ABOVE: Inside the Savoy, dancers like Ricky Babbit and Lucy Simms perfected the moves of the latest dance craze—the jitterbug.

ABOVE: Cooperstown, the supposed birthplace of baseball, was the obvious choice for the Baseball Hall of Fame. Local resident Abner Doubleday is said to have invented a rudimentary form of the game here, though most historians now agree that this is a popular myth. The museum opened its doors in June 1939 and now welcomes over 350,000 visitors each year. Joe DiMaggio (pictured) received his plaque on July 29, 1955.

ABOVE RIGHT: Prom Night was the highlight of the school year. In 1956, students of Horace Greeley High School in Chappaqua kicked up their heels to live music and celebrated the coming of summer and the end of high school.

RIGHT: Fire Island has long been a resort where you can relax and not worry too much about what the rest of the world thinks, as these ladies demonstrate in the 1950s. The first hotel on the island went up in 1880. By the time this photo was taken Fire Island was connected to Long Island by the Captree Causeway, making it much easier to visit.

ABOVE: The spread of roads around New York set the scene for new indus-
tries and entertainments. Probably the most famous of these, and one that
will be fondly remembered by many New Yorkers, was the drive-in movie.
The first of these opened on Sunrise Highway in Valley Stream, Long Island.
The twelve-acre tract accommodated 500 cars for a single showing.

NEW YORK SPORT

New York has many claims to fame, but perhaps its proudest is that it invented baseball as we know it today. The game actually originated in England, where it was called "rounders." There is a popular legend that Abner Doubleday devised the American version of the game here in Cooperstown, but it was actually Alexander Joy Cartwright who first developed the modern baseball field for his New York Knickerbocker Base Ball Club in 1845 and set new rules for the game.

These days, New York is very much a baseball state, boasting numerous teams including the major league Yankees and Mets as well as minor league teams like the Binghamton Mets, Brooklyn Cyclones, Syracuse Chiefs, and Jamestown Jammers among many others.

Many of its heroes were homegrown, like legendary Brooklyn Dodgers pitcher Johnny Podres, who lived his entire life in the upstate town of Glens Falls, New York. But it's not just in baseball that New York sports has led the way. The state fields

ABOVE: Oyster Bay on Long Island has a rich nautical history. It was here that the infamous Captain Kidd weighed anchor for the last time before sailing to Boston, where he was arrested and shipped to Britain to be hanged. The town has also been popular with yachting enthusiasts over the years and boasts one of New York's best clubs.

"There was a great, dark mystery about it when I first came here from Oklahoma. I still get goose pimples just walking inside it. Now I think this is about the prettiest ballpark I ever saw."

Mickey Mantle (on the original Yankee Stadium)

ABOVE: Competitors in the unofficial 1894 Amateur at St. Andrew's in Yonkers, only six years after golf had been introduced to the state. In later years the course would become one of the most famous in the world. St. Andrew's membership has included some of New York's most illustrious names, such as Andrew Carnegie and the revered pilot Eddie Rickenbacker.

BELOW: Vassar College founded women's baseball in 1866 and went on to field great teams of "bloomer girls." The young women of the college also enjoyed less formal games between themselves, such as this impromptu one on Class Day, 1928.

teams and hosts competitions of many kinds, and a large proportion of its citizens have long participated in one sport or another, even if it was just an impromptu game of sidewalk roller hockey.

Baseball isn't the only game New York has introduced to the United States. As you might expect for a state that has an Atlantic shoreline as well as access to the Great Lakes and its own smaller lakes, boating was a very popular early pastime. The New York Yacht Club, founded in 1844, was the first of its kind in the country and organized yacht racing off Manhattan Island as well as summer cruises, events that the club still sponsors.

The famous Saratoga Racecourse began thoroughbred horse races in 1863 and has been drawing thousands of race fans every summer since. Often nicknamed "The Graveyard of Favorites," the historic track is believed to be the oldest sporting facility of any kind still operating in the country.

The New York Tennis Club opened in 1886 in fields at 180th Street and Amsterdam Avenue and was—again—the first in the country. Two years later, in 1888, a Scottish gentleman named John Reid and a handful of friends met at a

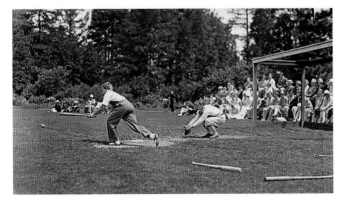

meadow in Yonkers and improvised a three-hole golf course. With an apple tree as their "clubhouse," they founded the St. Andrew's Golf Club, the first of many on the continent. New York also played a role in the formation of American football. It was here that delegates from the rugby/soccer-playing universities met to agree on a universal set of rules for their

ABOVE: Mildred "Babe" Didrikson, the Texas golf star, drives off at a charity golf match at Fresh Meadow Country Club, Long Island, in 1937. America's first female golf celebrity, she was paired in this match with Babe Ruth. They played against John Montague, Hollywood's mystery golfer, and Sylvia Annenberg, one of the best women players in the East. The match ended when the crowd invaded the ninth green and grabbed the balls as souvenirs.

ABOVE: Horse racing at Saratoga Springs has been one of New York State's prime attractions since the course opened here in 1863. These days it is the oldest organized sporting ground of any kind still operating in the United States.

RIGHT: Saratoga stable boys polish saddles in preparation for the opening of the racing season.

own version of the old English games in 1873. Since then, the state has fielded some of the greatest teams in history, including the world-famous Giants, who played their first game in New York City in 1925, and the Jets who were founded as the New York Titans in 1960. New Yorkers try to ignore the fact that both teams now play in New Jersey.

Winter sports were popular too, and New York State's mountains provided the perfect locations for skiing and tobogganing. So perfect in fact, that the Winter Olympics have been held at Lake Placid in the Adirondacks twice, in 1932 and again in 1980. The 1932 games welcomed athletes from seventeen nations and included skiing events as well as speed skating, figure skating, dog sledding, and thrills and spills on the bobsled run.

And it's not just the men who participated. Even in less enlightened times, New York's females were avid sportswomen. Tennis was popular, but women participated in most sports, including bicycle racing, rowing, hockey, and even baseball. The pioneering women at Vassar College created the first women's baseball team in 1861 and—despite raised eyebrows—set off a trend

RIGHT: Bernard Baruch, Wall Street financier and U.S. financial adviser, and Kitty Carlisle, singing star of the stage and screen, watch the races at Saratoga. Miss Carlisle was a regular at the track and spent her evenings at the Spa Theater there where she played the leading role in *Tonight or Never*.

RIGHT: Members of the Mohawk Golf Club Curling Team proudly display their brooms, stones, and curious choice of headgear in 1920, shortly before they went on to glory, winning the W. F. Allen Medal at Utica.

that swept the country. The so-called "Bloomer Girl" teams took their name from the loose pants created for them by Amelia Bloomer. By the 1960s women across the country had also started playing football, though it wasn't until over thirty years later that the Women's Professional Football League was formed. In 1999, the all-female New York Sharks became the first national champions after beating the Minnesota Vixens 12–6.

New York's best loved game is baseball, and nowhere epitomizes the state's love affair with the game more than Yankee Stadium in the Bronx. Probably the world's most famous ballpark, it was the home of the New York Yankees, affectionately known as the Bronx Bombers, from 1923 until 2008 when a replacement stadium was built next

UP WHERE WINTER
≈ CALLS TO PLAY ≈

OLYMPIC
BOBSLED RUN
OPERATED BY N.Y. STATE CONSERVATION DEPT.
LAKE PLACID

OPPOSITE: Spectators line up to watch high-speed action on the bobsled run at the 1932 Lake Placid Olympics. The American four-man team of Fiske, Eagan, Gray, and O'Brien send up a shower of snow as they complete their gold medal winning run.

LEFT: A 1932 poster advertises the Olympic bobsled run at Lake Placid.

BELOW: Skiers at the busy winter resort of Lake Placid in 1929. The Adirondacks have been luring winter sports fans since the 1880s. Close-by Saranac Lake hosted the area's first ski competitions in 1889.

door. New York's other major league team, the Mets, played in Shea Stadium in Queens from 1963 to 2008 and, like their rivals, the Yankees, also started the 2009 season in a new stadium next door to the old one. During its long and illustrious lifetime, Yankee Stadium hosted thirty-seven World Series and made an indelible impression on the millions of Yankee fans who watched their team play there over the years. Appropriately the Yankees won both the first and last games ever played at the stadium (beating the Boston Red Sox 4–1 on April 18, 1923, and the Baltimore Orioles 7–3 on September 21, 2008).

These are just a few of the events, places, and times that have contributed to New York's sporting heritage. Add some of history's greatest arenas, such as Madison Square Garden, which hosted notable boxing matches including the 1971 Ali-Frazier fight; speedways such as the Shangri-La in Oswego and the Chemung Speedrome; and stadiums catering to everything from equestrian sports (the Lake Placid Equestrian Center) to college football, and you get some idea of just what a sporting state New York is.

YANKEE STADIUM

ABOVE: Yankee Stadium on Opening Day—April 18, 1923. At the ceremonies a brass band played and Babe Ruth was presented with a baseball bat. The first ball was thrown by New York governor Alfred E. Smith.

RIGHT: Lou Gehrig of the Yankees hits a three-bagger during a game against Washington at Yankee Stadium in July 1927.

The Bronx's original Yankee Stadium, which opened in 1923, delighted baseball fans for eighty-five years. In that time the Yankees played 6,581 home games there, with some of the sport's greatest players taking the field. Fans have witnessed many of baseball's most famous moments, including nine games that clinched the World Series for the Yankees. During its lifetime, the stadium was also used for boxing matches, football games, and rock concerts, and several popes even celebrated Mass there. With so many memories attached to the park, it's no wonder the stadium has a special place in New York's heritage.

LEFT: Brooklyn Dodgers fans give their own version of the Bronx "cheer" at Yankee Stadium, where the Dodgers clashed with the New York Yankees in the first game of the World Series in 1941. To the Dodgers dismay, the Yankees prevailed once again that year. Dodger fans had to wait until 1955 to finally beat the Yankees in what everyone called a "New York subway series."

LEFT: For many sports fans, Yankee Stadium was about more than just baseball. Numerous other events were hosted there, including this football match between the New York Yanks and Los Angeles Rams in 1950.

RIGHT: The New York Giants' Charlie Conerly (left) passes against the Baltimore Colts at Yankee Stadium on December 28, 1958.

OPPOSITE: Another of New York's grand old ballparks was Ebbets Field in Brooklyn, home of the Brooklyn Dodgers until 1957, the year that the Dodgers broke Brooklyn's heart by moving to Los Angeles. It was demolished three years later, a sad loss for baseball and the city, as well as for boys who knew the best places to find a free seat.

ABOVE LEFT: While it may not have quite the same place in New York mythology as Yankee Stadium, for many (including the author) Shea Stadium was held in just as high esteem. Home to the Mets from 1963 to 2008, it filled the holes left in many Brooklyn hearts when the Dodgers moved to Los Angeles. In 1968, there were few more loyal fans than the nuns of Brooklyn's St. Joseph's Convent, though having God on their side didn't help the Mets for this particular game. They lost 2–1 to the Cubs.

LEFT: In the days when they were barred from many team sports, the girls of New York often demonstrated their athletic abilities in beautifully choreographed support. Cheerleading became so popular that competitions between rival teams began, such as the annual cheerleading contest in Fordham University's gymnasium in the Bronx.

RIGHT: New York City was also the birthplace of one of the country's favorite pastimes. The first bowling alley in the United States—Knickerbockers in New York City—opened in 1840. The modern rules were formulated by the American Bowling Congress, which was also based in the city, in 1895. Bowling alleys, such as the McClean Bowl-O-Drome in Yonkers, seen here in 1941, reached their pinnacle of popularity in the 1950s, but many still have their loyal fans.

RIGHT: Many sports have had their origins in New York, and among them might be counted Jet-skiing. This early model —called the "water skipper"—was demonstrated on the Hudson in 1955 by Otto Hassold and his assistant Terry Allen.

RIGHT: Not all sports needed a fancy stadium or equipment, and young New Yorkers were inventive enough to improvise when necessary. An "ice" hockey game, for example, could quite easily be organized with just a few pairs of strap-on roller skates, an old crate, and the sidewalk.

OPPOSITE: One of the most famous boxing matches in history was dubbed "The Fight of the Century" and pitted Joe Frazier against Muhammad Ali at Madison Square Garden in March 1971. After fifteen grueling rounds, during which Ali struggled to stay on his feet, the judges handed the fight to Frazier. The two would meet twice more and Ali would win both matches.

TOP RIGHT: College sports have a long and proud heritage in New York, as you'd expect from a state that has some of the country's finest universities. Cornell's national championship crew gets an early season briefing from Coach Harrison Sanford prior to a workout on Cayuga Lake in 1956.

RIGHT: Stanford University also has a proud heritage of rowing and has produced Olympic gold medalists on numerous occasions. In 1913, the team trained on the Hudson River, near Poughkeepsie.

A SPECIAL PLACE

For many first-time visitors to New York City, walking down Fifth Avenue or Broadway is like returning to a place they've known all their life. For a century or more the Big Apple has been seen in photographs, art, and movies all around the world. It's been celebrated in song and been the subject of literature. More recently, its streets have been on television screens everywhere, courtesy of shows from *Taxi* to *Friends*. All over the world, people instantly recognize the Empire State Building, can tell you what color a New York taxi is, and know the best places to shop without ever consulting a tourist guide. There is no getting away from the fact that the city's fame has eclipsed that of its home state, and that's understandable, for it is a city that thoroughly deserves its title of the "Unofficial Capital of the World." But for native New Yorkers and the many millions of tourists who have ventured off Manhattan Island, New York City is just a gem in a golden setting, a setting which is just as rich and

ABOVE: Despite its reputation as a state where new technologies are invented and business deals are struck, New York has a rich farming heritage that continues to this day with a progressive attitude to locally grown food. These days, the Farmers' Museum in Cooperstown pays tribute to the often over-looked men, women, and children who have fed the state for centuries.

"Each man reads his own meaning into New York."

Meyer Berger

OPPOSITE, BOTTOM: In the late nineteenth and early twentieth century, newspapers were sold by chil-dren—the "newsboys" or "newsies"—whose shouts of "extra extra" were part of life on the streets of every city. Often poor or homeless and unable to return unsold copies, the youngsters went on strike in 1899 and crippled the circulation of New York's papers for two weeks before newspaper magnates agreed to buy back remaining papers.

ABOVE: New York State is a treasure trove of rural scenic delights including covered bridges like this one at Riders Mill.

beautiful, and every bit as alluring as the dazzling spires of the city.

No one is quite sure why New York is called the "Empire State." Some believe it's because George Washington once called it "the seat of empire." Others attribute it to the state's early reputation for wealth and resources. Whatever the reason, the name has stuck, emblazoned not only on the famous skyscraper, but also on every automobile license plate and countless business signs throughout the state. And everyone has a share in its history. In one way or another and in one place or another—from Albany to Buffalo and the tip of Long Island to the northern border with Canada—New York State has touched the lives of billions of people who have come here, and billions more who could only imagine it.

Not many states have the same name as their largest city, but New Yorkers are quick to define themselves as residents of either "upstate"—north or west of the city—or "downstate"—in or around the city. While their accents and lifestyles may be different, they are all proud to call themselves New Yorkers. And they have much to be proud of. Other cities can rival the skyline of New York State's most

ABOVE: Sunlight streaming into Grand Central Station. The fabulous Beaux-Arts–style terminus opened in 1913 and served several railroad companies. It was also directly responsible for the surge in construction in the area (including the Chrysler Building) and was a small city in its own right, housing stores and restaurants including the famous Grand Central Oyster Bar, which opened with the station in 1913 and is still serving fine seafood today.

famous metropolis. Chicago, for instance, has skyscrapers taller than the Empire State. A few regions could claim higher mountains or prettier scenery. Still more could bid for the position of business and technology capital of the world. Some might even claim a richer cultural heritage or grander museums. Yet New York has a unique appeal, perhaps because the state has all these things, and more.

In his book, *Downtown*, published a few years after the tragedy of September 11, 2001, native New Yorker and writer Pete Hamill calls New York the "capital of nostalgia," the place of constant change where everyone realizes that nothing stays the same. The images in the book you hold now both prove and challenge that belief. They illustrate the way we were and the way we are in New York.

The lives and times of New Yorkers haven't always been easy and the hardships faced by pioneers and immigrants—as well as more recent challenges—have forged a formidable character. Indeed, much has been written about New Yorkers' courage and grit in the face of adversity as well as their unique humor. New York isn't just the creation of architects, planners, and politicians, or even builders, canal diggers,

RIGHT: A view down State Street in Albany toward the Hudson around 1920. The distinctive Gothic, red-roofed building at the foot of the street could be taken for a state capitol, but is actually the newly finished Delaware & Hudson and *Albany Evening Standard* Building.

BELOW: Not every great building in New York is in Manhattan. Many, such as the Syracuse Savings Bank standing next to the Erie Canal, give the smaller cities of New York a metropolitan charm all their own. Completed in 1876, the bank was the tallest building in the city and also the first with an elevator, which allowed visitors to ride in ease and comfort up the tower to enjoy views over one of the state's busiest crossroad cities.

RIGHT: Shoeshining has long been a busy trade across New York State. Among those who have earned their living polishing shoes was Malcolm X, who worked as a bootblack at the Lindy Hop nightclub in New York City, in the days before he became a political leader. Here in Watertown, bootblack Joe Forting administers a shine to New York governor Averell Harriman's shoes in 1958.

FAR RIGHT: As this family in Westchester demonstrates in 1952, the warm summers of New York State are perfect for lying around in the shade.

BOTTOM: Three hikers take in the spectacular views from the peak of Mount Morris in the Adirondacks, looking toward Tupper Lake—scenery to rival any in the world.

LEFT: As well as attracting traditional tourists, New York City has always been a magnet for thinkers, radicals, artists, beatniks, and musicians. From the Forties onward, most gravitated toward Greenwich Village where Café Bizarre became a popular haunt.

BELOW: Pedestrians stroll beneath neon lights in a New York City snowstorm in 1932. In every season and in every type of weather, the city has an undeniable charisma.

railway workers, or road layers; it's been built by countless people, over hundreds of years. The people of New York—many of them pictured in the different eras and activities shown in this book—also deserve credit for shaping New York the way it was and the way it is today.

Those long-ago pioneers, immigrants, and new arrivals from other parts of the country have all added something to their chosen home, and the state has benefited from becoming a heady mixture of peoples and cultures from just about every corner of the planet. Whether their ancestors came from Africa, Europe, Asia, or anywhere else, the diverse people who have lived here have woven a fabric that is stronger and more colorful than many of them could have imagined. In return the state was kind to them. For many the promise of a better life was filled, and for those whose times were harder there was always hope to be found. The knowledge that there were good times ahead for those who gave their best has given both the city and the state a forward-thinking frame of mind. Although its citizens have been through some tough times together, New York has always come back, adding more to its history and polishing its name ever brighter.

OPPOSITE (ABOVE AND BELOW): In the days before suburban malls and supermarkets, New Yorkers depended on local stores. Small town centers were vibrant places where neighbors could catch up on gossip while shopping and, by the Thirties and Forties, refresh themselves at a soda fountain.

LEFT: In New York City, even the most simple everyday scenes have a timeless nostalgic charm. This photograph of a businessman getting coffee in one of the city's diners dates to the 1960s, but so little has changed over the years that it could have been taken yesterday.

BELOW: Hot dog vendors plying their trade, one of New York City's most enduring sights. Though the Big Apple may be best known for the Statue of Liberty, its street life, personalities, sights, and sounds are what has given it a unique personality.

ABOVE: New York is, of course, "the city that never sleeps," a city where celebrities enjoy the high life alongside the everyday world. Exemplifying the thrills of New York City life, the beautiful Marilyn Monroe tries to hold down her dress as wind from a subway grate blows it upward during filming of *The Seven Year Itch* in Manhattan.

RIGHT: Movie directors have long exploited the city's great architecture and gritty feel as backdrops to their work. As an unpaid star the Big Apple has appeared in motion pictures ranging from *King Kong* to *Independence Day*. One of the greatest is Woody Allen's *Manhattan*. Diane Keaton and Allen take a break on the ready-made set in 1979.

LEFT AND BELOW: Often referred to as the "Crossroads of the World," New York City's famous Times Square has for many years been a gathering place at times of celebration. Under sparkling neon lights New Yorkers have welcomed presidents, brought in the new year, and partied after a World Series. These scenes from VE Day—May 7, 1945—show the surging crowd's joy at the unofficial publication of Germany's unconditional surrender. Despite the lack of confirmation of victory, New York went wild with its usual barrage of ticker tape and torn paper. And, of course, there was kissing.

PAGES 126–127: New York City sparkles in the early darkness of a 1973 New York night. Close to the center are the newly finished towers of the World Trade Center, an integral part of the famous skyline for twenty-eight years.

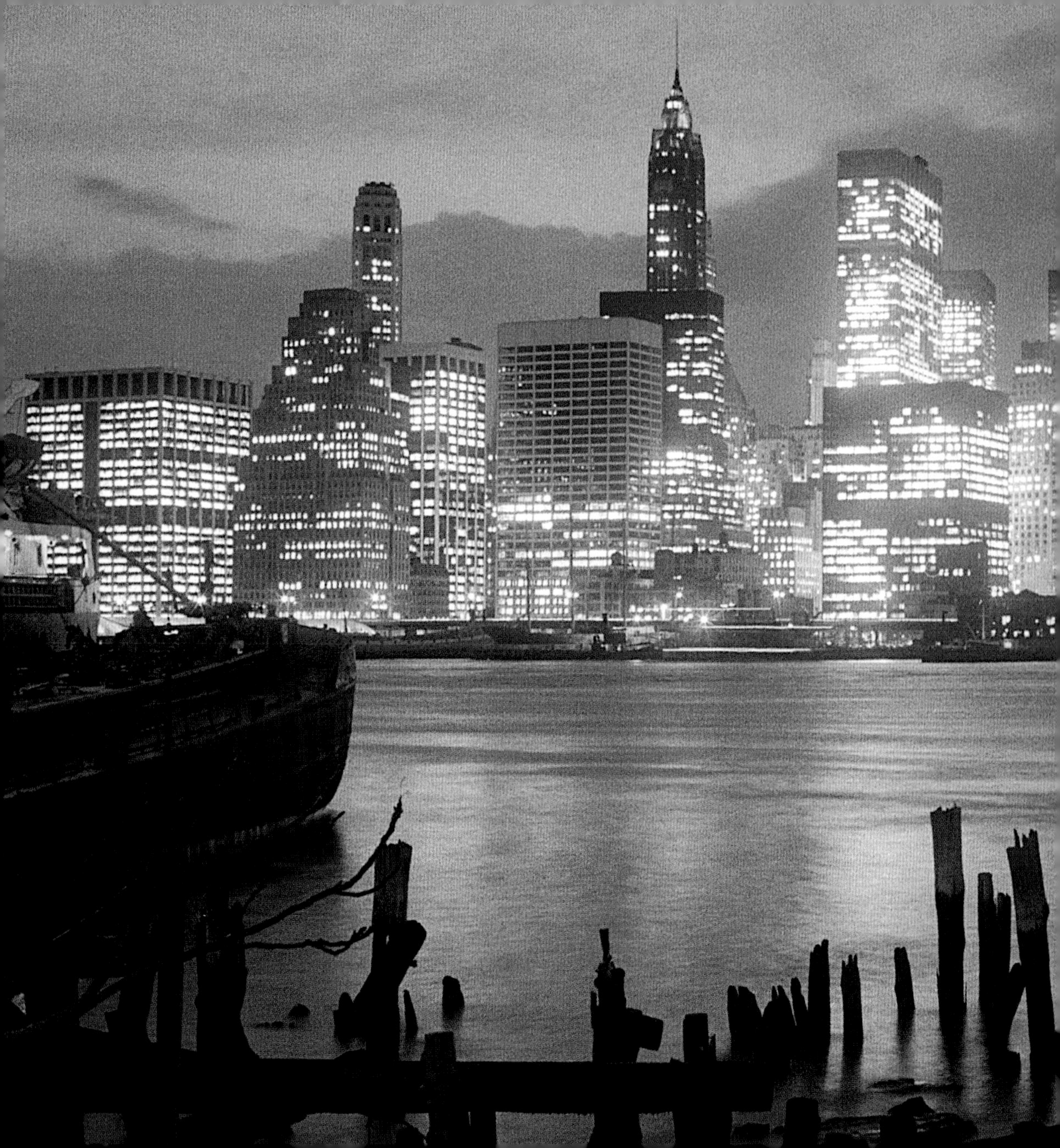

References in **bold** refer to illustrations.

Adirondacks, 22, **85**
African-Americans, 12
airports, **52**, **53**
Albany, **10**, **11**, **12**, **13**, **42–43**, 119
Ali, Muhammad, **114**
architecture, 8, 60–68, **78**. See also Levittown
automobiles, 22

Babbit, Ricky, **95**
Baruch, Bernard, **102**
baseball, **96**, 98, **98**, **99**, 102, 106–109
Baseball Hall of Fame, **96**
beaches, **37**
The Beatles, **53**
Big Apple, **124–125**
boating, 99
bobsled, **104**
bowling, **112**
boxing, **114**
bridges, **31**, **34–35**, 117
Broadway, **88**, **89**
Brooklyn Bridge, **34–35**
Buffalo, **9**, 15, 18, **20–21**, **23**, **42–3**, 51, 64, 88, 90, 92

camping, **85**
Capri Village, **86–87**
Carlisle, Kitty, **102**
Cartwright, Alexander J., 98
Catskill Aqueduct, **40**
Catskill Mountains, 17, 21, **40**, **84**
Central Park, **90–91**, 30, 32
Chatham, **8**
cheerleading, **111**
children, **46**, 51, **70**, 78, **81**, 87, 101, 110, **112–113**, 117
Chrysler Building, **25**, 27, **38**
Conerly, Charlie, **108–109**
Coney Island, 36, **36**, **37**

Cooperstown, **96**
Cornell University, 13
Cotton Club, **89**
Curtiss, Glenn, **52**

dances, 94, **94–95**
Delta Lake Dam, **43**
DeWitt Clinton, 44, **48**
Didrikson, Mildred "Babe," **100**
Dodgers, **108**
Dreamland, **37**
drive-in movies, **97**

East River, **46**
Ebbets Field, **110**
Electric Tower, **23**
electricity, 48–49. See also General Electric Company
"Empire State," 117–118
Empire State Building, **26**, **38**, 38, **39**
entertainment, 80
Erie Canal, 12, 15, 41, 43–44, **44**

farming, **116**
festivals, 22, **92**
Finger Lakes, **20**
Fire Island, **22**, **96**
firefighters, **58**
Flatiron Building, **14**, **27**
football, 100, 102
Fort Amsterdam, 9, 40
Frazier, Joe, **114**

gas stations, **55**
Gehrig, Lou, **106**
General Electric Company, 56, **56**, **57**, **72**, **73**
Giants, **108–109**
golf, **99**, 100, **100**
Grand Central Station, **118**
Grand Union Hotel, **29**
Great Depression, 64, **65**

Hamill, Pete, 118
Hamilton Fish Park, **84–85**

Harriman, Averell, **120**
hiking, **120**
home appliance, **71**, **72**, **73**
horse racing, 99, **101**
hot dog vendors, **123**
houses. See architecture
Huntington, **82**
hydrant spray, **59**

ice hockey, **112–113**
ice storm, **58**
immigrants, 7
interior design, **74**, **75**, **76**, **79**

Jerome B. Rice & Co., **41**
jet-skiing, **112**
jitterbug, **95**

"Lady Liberty," **33**
Lake George, **86–87**
Lake Minnewaska, **84**
Lake Placid Olympics, **104**, **105**
Lake Erie, **42–43**
Levittown, 66, **68**, 68, **69**
Lind, Jenny, 18

Madison Square, **26–27**
Madison Square Garden, **114**
The Maid of the Mist, **21**
Manhattan Bridge, **31**
markets, **12**
Martin House, Darwin D., 60, **63**
McKinley, William, 22
Met Life Tower, **27**
Mitchel, John P., **31**
"Modern Venus Contest 1937," **83**
Mohawk Golf Club, **103**
Monroe, Marilyn, **124**
Mount Morris, **120**
moving pictures, 80, **81**
music, **94**, 94

Native tribes, 6, 11
New York City, 18, 47–48, 116, **121**, **126–127**

naming of, 11–12
traffic, **54–55**
New Yorkers, 117, 118, 121
Newburgh, **62**
newsboys, **117**
Niagara Falls, **19**, **21**
nightclubs, **92**
nuns, **111**

Oehl, Sidney, **77**
Olympics, **104**, **105**
Oyster Bay, **98**

Pan-American Exposition, 22, **23**
picnic, **85**
Pieter Bronck House, **61**
proms, **96**
public services, 51–52

railways, 44, 47
restaurants, **15**, 88, **91**, **122–123**
Roosevelt, Theodore, 22
rowhouses, **64**
rowing, **115**

sailing, **98**
Saratoga Springs, 28, **28**, **29**, **101**
Savage's Hotel and Casino, **83**
Shaker house, **63**
Shea Stadium, **111**
shoeshining, **120**
Simms, Lucy, **95**
Singer Building, **26**
skiing, **105**
skyscrapers, **24–27**, **32**, **38**, **39**
snowstorm, **121**
springs, **28**
St. Andrew, **99**
state capitol, **11**
stores, **122**
streetcars, **47**, **48**
subway, 48, **50–51**
swing bands, 94, **94**
Syracuse Savings Bank, **119**

television services, **71**

tennis, 99, 102
Thanksgiving Day Parade, **93**
theaters, 18, 21, 82, **82**, 88–90
Times Square, **125**
tourist industry, 18
trains, 48, **49**, 50
Tupper Lake, **120**

VE Day celebration, **125**

Washington Square Arch, **31**
water, 49
Wilcox, Richard, **66–67**
wireless broadcasting, **91**
women, **56**, 99, **100**, 102, **111**, **112**
Woolworth Building, **24**
Wright, Frank Lloyd, 60, **63**

Yankee Stadium, 102, 105, **106–109**
Yankees, **106–107**, **108**